CounterCultural
Christians

Exploring a Christian Worldview

with

Charles Colson

PARTICIPANT GUIDE

by Tracey D. Lawrence

Loveland, Colorado

Group's
R.E.A.L.
Guarantee
to you:

This Group resource incorporates our R.E.A.L. approach to ministry— one that encourages long-term retention and life transformation. It's ministry that's:

RELATIONAL
Because learner-to-learner interaction enhances learning and builds Christian friendships.

EXPERIENTIAL
Because what learners experience through discussion and action sticks with them up to 9 times longer than what they simply hear or read.

APPLICABLE
Because the aim of Christian education is to equip learners to be both hearers and doers of God's Word.

LEARNER-BASED
Because learners understand and retain more when the learning process takes into consideration how they learn best.

CounterCultural Christians: Exploring a Christian Worldview With Charles Colson
PARTICIPANT GUIDE

Visit our Web site: **www.grouppublishing.com**

CREDITS

THE WILBERFORCE FORUM:
Charles W. Colson, chairman of Prison Fellowship Ministries and The Wilberforce Forum
Nigel M. de S. Cameron, Ph.D., executive editor
Tracey D. Lawrence, project manager and writer

BREAKPOINT WITH *Chuck Colson*
Jim Tonkowich, managing editor
Roberto Rivera, writer
Anne Morse, writer
A special thank you to the Wilberforce Forum staff for all their efforts and individual dedication that went toward producing this product.

GROUP PUBLISHING, INC.:
Beth Rowland, editor
Matt Lockhart, creative development editor
Joani Schultz, chief creative officer
Janis Sampson, copy editor
Jean Bruns, book designer
Pat Miller and Joyce Douglas, print production artists
Jeff A. Storm, cover art director/designer
Daniel Treat, cover photography
Peggy Naylor, production manager

ISBN 0-7644-2522-6
10 9 8 7 6 5 4 3 2   11 10 09 08 07 06 05 04 03
Printed in the United States of America.

CONTENTS

This book is dedicated to my loving family, who consistently prove to me it is possible to live as true disciples for Christ in the twenty-first century. Noel, my husband and friend, thank you for your willingness to shepherd our small group and for the eternal investment you have made in each of us. Your journey with God is a beautiful thing to behold. Mom and Dad, your unswerving faith and resilience continue to inspire me to press on toward the Goal. Kevin, I thank you for the ingenious ways you live out your life and faith. I am proud to call you my brother. You are all God's gift to me in this life and the life to come.

With gratitude,
Tracey D. Lawrence

Each session in this study is designed to help participants learn what it means to look at the world through the lens of Christianity. The sessions accomplish this through discussion, through study, and through relationship with the others in the group. Here's a breakdown of how each session is structured.

GETTING STARTED *(15 minutes)*

The warm-up activity will introduce participants to the session topic. The group will participate in a fun, nonthreatening activity together and will then have a discussion about their experience. Participants will be encouraged to build relationships, to share of themselves, and to begin to think about the day's topic.

A VIEW OF OUR WORLD *(30 minutes)*

BREAKPOINT EXERCISE

In this activity participants will listen to and discuss a Break-Point radio broadcast narrated by Chuck Colson. These broadcast segments are on the CD in the *CounterCultural Christians* kit.

CULTURE WATCH

Next, participants will watch and discuss a video segment from the video found in the *CounterCultural Christians* kit. In these video segments, Chuck Colson will give the group more information about the day's topic.

QUOTE, UNQUOTE

Then participants will read and discuss a quotation that relates to the day's topic.

THE VIEW FROM SCRIPTURE *(30 minutes)*

At this point the group will dig into the Scriptures to see what the Bible says about the day's topic and developing a Christian worldview.

WRAPPING UP *(15 minutes)*

This section includes a closing activity to challenge and encourage participants to draw conclusions from what they've learned and to put it into practice. There is also a time for group prayer.

A VIEW OF YOUR WORLD

In this section, participants will be encouraged to do something during the week that will help them apply what they've learned to their own life situations. Participants will be asked to report on what they did and on what they learned at the beginning of the next session.

W e live in times when our faith is deeply informed and influenced by the trends of our culture. Somehow we have reversed God's foundational absolutes: Christ should be influencing culture, rather than our culture influencing Christianity. "Cultural Christianity" is a term used to express the negative impact our culture has had on the core beliefs of Christianity. We don't have to look far to realize that Christians aren't responding much differently than non-Christians to issues we face in all matters of life and practice. Thus, to our critics, our faith can appear to be impotent. If we do not understand how Christianity should influence our entire lives, we become easy prey to the cultural whims of pop culture.

This study is designed to equip and encourage Christians to live out their faith in all platforms of life. The Wilberforce Forum, a division of Prison Fellowship, seeks to foster the renewal of culture with a worldview apologetic, reaching the church with this call to the public square. Participants will be challenged with Chuck Colson's plea to contend for the truth in modern society with compelling video segments and selected BreakPoint radio transcripts.

It is vital that we begin to understand the need to think *Christianly*—which means more than piously. Our message to the world is that God's revelation is the source of all truth; it is the core for understanding all of reality.

Through this study The Wilberforce Forum wishes to challenge Christians to move their faith from an internal, personal understanding of salvation toward an outward, world-conscious understanding that reaches all facets of culture. During this twelve-week study, you will explore popular worldviews that oppose a Christian worldview, taking a closer look at how any worldview profoundly impacts the sciences, the arts, education, and entertainment. The goal is for us to teach others to see that what is good and true is unreachable without God and that we must add God's truth to all subject matters.

We pray that you find meaningful ways that God may be specifically calling you to be a countercultural Christian. We encourage you to take your faith way beyond John 3:16 and transform the world around you.

"He is before all things, and in him all things hold together" (Colossians 1:17).

Honoring You in Christ Jesus,
Tracey D. Lawrence

How Do I See the World?

GETTING STARTED *(15 minutes)*

Introduce yourself and share with the group the last movie you saw or a movie that has deeply impacted you. Explain why you liked or didn't like the movie. Discuss these questions:

• Were redemptive themes or destructive themes shown in the movie? Explain.

• Did you sense there was a clear message that the producers and writers wanted to communicate?

• How do movies and other forms of popular culture present a particular way of viewing the world?

Today's lesson discusses the idea of worldview. Our worldview is simply the way we view the world. It's shaped by our beliefs about all aspects of life and the world around us. Our worldview ultimately guides our daily decisions and actions.

A View of Our World *(30 minutes)*

BreakPoint Exercise

LISTEN TO TRACK 1 OF THE CD. In this BreakPoint segment, which aired December 21, 2001, Chuck Colson discusses how the Christian worldview of J.R.R. Tolkien shaped the content of *The Lord of the Rings*.

• How did *The Lord of the Rings* emphasize and promote a Christian view of the world?

• In what ways does *The Lord of the Rings* "afford us an opportunity to tell others about the centrality of the Christian faith"?

Culture Watch

WATCH VIDEO SEGMENT 1. In this video segment, Chuck Colson explains why Christians should be concerned about worldview.

• What non-Christian worldviews compete for our attention? How do they do that?

• Do non-Christian worldviews pose a threat to Christianity? Why or why not?

"Without a biblical worldview, all the great teaching goes in one ear and out the other. There are no intellectual pegs...in the mind of the individual to hang these truths on. So they just pass through. They don't stick. They don't make a difference."
—GEORGE BARNA

Read the quotation from George Barna, and discuss these questions:

• Do you agree with Barna? Why or why not? Do you see this happening in our culture today?

• What great teachings are being ignored in our culture today?

• How can the way we see the world change our experience of the world? How does it affect our decisions? our career choices?

THE VIEW FROM SCRIPTURE *(30 minutes)*

Read Matthew 4:1-11 aloud.

1. Do you see the temptations Jesus faced evident in our culture? Explain.

2. How did Satan cleverly disguise evil into seemingly good things for Jesus to desire? How is that similar to or different from how non-Christian worldviews entice us away from a Christian understanding of the world around us?

3. How did Jesus' worldview help him refute Satan?

4. How did Jesus' view of Scripture affect the outcome of the story?

5. How does our view of Scripture affect our worldview? How does a Christian worldview develop?

6. Sometimes Christians separate the sacred from the secular in their lives. What happens when Christians see their faith as just one component of life instead of being pervasive?

7. What should or shouldn't be part of a Christian worldview? Should all Christians agree about worldview? Explain.

WRAPPING UP *(15 minutes)*

Find a partner, and look through a magazine, a newspaper, or even the Yellow Pages of the phone book. Look for the influence of both a Christian worldview and a non-Christian worldview. Discuss why worldview matters to the Christian. Talk about how you can be aware of worldview and how that awareness should affect your daily life.

Come back together as a group and discuss your discoveries.

PRAYER TIME

CLOSE YOUR SESSION IN PRAYER. Be sure to take the time to pray for each other. You may want to list prayer requests below so you can pray for each other during the week.

A VIEW OF YOUR WORLD

During the week watch a movie with a friend and identify the worldview behind the movie. Do you feel that more than one worldview is presented? What, if any, biblical themes can be identified? Did the movie have a positive or negative message?

Can Christianity and Science Coexist?

GETTING STARTED *(15 minutes)*

Form groups of two to four, and observe the flower your leader gives you. Use all your senses to examine and record its characteristics. Then come back together, and discuss as a large group the uniqueness and complexity of the flowers; for example, you might describe how they grow, what their role is in nature, and their different fragrances.

• How does your faith in God affect how you perceive the flower? Would a person who doesn't believe in God perceive the flower differently? Explain.

Then in your pair or foursome discuss your high school biology class.

• Was there a place in your high school biology class for any discussion of faith, God, or Christianity? Explain your experience.

• Are faith and science mutually exclusive or can they coexist or even complement each other?

THE VIEW REVIEWED

Tell the rest of the group what insights you gained from doing the "View of Your World" activity from the last lesson.

A VIEW OF OUR WORLD *(30 minutes)*

BREAKPOINT EXERCISE

LISTEN TO TRACK 2 OF THE CD. In this BreakPoint segment, which aired June 3, 1992, Chuck Colson discusses how a Christian worldview has influenced science.

• How has it happened that the relationship between science and faith has changed from friendly to combative?

• How should a Christian view science?

CULTURE WATCH

WATCH VIDEO SEGMENT 2. In this video segment, Chuck Colson contrasts the idea of naturalism with a Christian view of science.

• Colson says, "When it comes to the origin of life, science is squarely on the side of creation by an intelligent agent." How do you respond to that statement? How would others (family, neighbors, co-workers) respond to that statement?

• Is there evidence in nature to support Colson's statement? Explain.

"A universe that is infinitely old requires no Creator...We are, in the most profound sense, children of the Cosmos."

—CARL SAGAN

"The Cosmos is all that there is or ever was or ever will be...Some part of our being knows this is from where we came. We long to return."

—CARL SAGAN

Read the quotations from Carl Sagan, and discuss these questions:

• Describe Sagan's worldview. Do Sagan's words seem more scientific or more philosophical?

• How might Sagan's worldview affect the way he interprets scientific data?

THE VIEW FROM SCRIPTURE *(30 minutes)*

Read Genesis 1:1 and Psalm 100:3.

1. How do these verses counter the idea of naturalism?

Read Job 38:1-18; 40:2-5; and Job 42:1-6.

2. Why does God explain all of this to Job? What difference did this dialogue make in Job's life?

3. How does the passage from Job support "intelligent design"? How does the idea of intelligent design differ from naturalism?

Read Romans 1:20.

4. What can we learn about God from observing nature?

5. How will a naturalistic worldview affect a person's life both day to day and ultimately? Are there any naturalistic tendencies in your own thought processes?

6. How does naturalism threaten or compromise a Christian worldview?

7. How can Christians thoughtfully and intelligently counter naturalism and promote a Christian understanding of science?

WRAPPING UP *(15 minutes)*

As a group, brainstorm things you learned in science class. See how many ideas you can come up with in three minutes. Then talk about what those science facts and theories reveal about God. Talk about how your view of God affects how you interpret science.

Share with a partner what you've learned in today's session and how it will change the way you look at science in your daily life.

CLOSE YOUR SESSION IN PRAYER. Be sure to take the time to pray for each other. You may want to list prayer requests below so you can pray for each other during the week.

A VIEW OF YOUR WORLD

Surf the Internet this week, and look at Web sites on intelligent design. Also search for Web sites that support evolution. Compare your findings. What assumptions of evolution oppose a Christian worldview?

Does Anything Matter?

GETTING STARTED *(15 minutes)*

As a group, discuss some of the bumper stickers you've seen that challenge your worldview. You may want to discuss bumper stickers such as these:

"My Kid Just Beat Up an Honor Student"

"Whoever Dies With the Most Toys Wins"

"Love Your Mother—Mother Earth, That Is"

• How do these messages show what our culture values?

• How should a Christian respond to the influence of such messages on our culture?

QUICK DEFINITION

Today's lesson discusses nihilism, which is the belief that life holds no meaning or purpose. Nihilism is more of an attitude than a philosophy. It denies everything—reality, beauty, morals, knowledge. "Whatever" is the pervading sentiment.

A VIEW OF OUR WORLD *(30 minutes)*

BREAKPOINT EXERCISE

LISTEN TO TRACK 3 OF THE CD. In this BreakPoint segment, which aired December 16, 1999, Chuck Colson discusses the deadly effects of nihilism.

• How did Harris and Klebold perceive the world around them? How did their beliefs influence their actions?

• Why do our youth struggle to make sense out of life? Why do they struggle to see life positively?

WATCH VIDEO SEGMENT 3. In this video segment, Chuck Colson explains nihilism and shows how it opposes a Christian worldview.

• Naturalism says that matter is all there is and we operate in a closed system, with no grid for God. Describe how naturalism logically leads to nihilism. You may want to go back and read the quotations from Carl Sagan on page 18.

• How does this worldview illustrate blatant rebellion against God?

QUOTE,
UNQUOTE

James Sire, author of *The Universe Next Door*, points out that nihilism is the natural child of naturalism. He summarizes the nihilists' argument, which says:

❝*Human beings are conscious machines without the ability to effect their own destiny or do anything significant; therefore, human beings (as valuable beings) are dead. There is no significance to any life for the nihilist.*❞

Read the quotation from James Sire, and discuss these questions:

• Where do you see evidence of nihilism in our culture?

• Friedrich Nietzsche, the German philosopher of the nineteenth century, asserted that "God is dead." What ramifications does this nihilistic view have on culture? on individuals?

THE VIEW FROM SCRIPTURE *(30 minutes)*

Read Genesis 1:26-27; Jeremiah 29:11; and Galatians 2:20.

1. In what ways do you struggle with finding meaning and significance in the day-to-day routines of life?

2. How does Christianity give us value and significance?

3. How does nihilism creep from secular culture into our Christian lives?

Read John 10:10 and Ephesians 3:17-21.

4. What does it mean to live an abundant life or a full life as a Christian? Do Christians really live abundant lives? Explain.

Read John 10:28 and 1 John 5:11-12.

5. Why is it important to connect our lives in the here and now with eternity? Are most Christians conscious of the fact that what happens in this life has eternal significance and consequence? Why or why not?

6. How does the reality of eternity give us hope?

7. How can we respond to those with a nihilistic worldview? How would our culture be different if people understood their God-given worth?

Wrapping Up *(15 minutes)*

Pretend that you are a nihilist. Spend two minutes brainstorming with the group about how you as nihilists view the world and your future in the world.

Next spend two minutes brainstorming with the group about how you as Christians view the world and your future in the world.

Then compare the two brainstorming sessions.

Discuss how Christians can be agents of hope in the world.

PRAYER TIME

CLOSE YOUR SESSION IN PRAYER. Be sure to take the time to pray for each other. You may want to list prayer requests below so you can pray for each other during the week.

A View of Your World

In light of your study on nihilism, spend time observing youth culture this week. You may want to visit your church's youth group, go to a mall, or watch TV. Reflect on what young people appear to be concerned with and their attitudes about their own self-worth. What do they talk about? What does their style of clothing communicate to you? Is there a significant difference between Christian and non-Christian teens?

What Is the Meaning of My Life?

GETTING STARTED *(15 minutes)*

Form groups of two to four, and define several of the following words: *rich, poor, hot, cold, sad, married, science, art, God, miracle*. Have at least two groups define each term. Compare your definitions.

• Did you all agree with the conclusions drawn in your group? Why or why not?

• Which terms seem to be more subjective or more objective? What personal experiences can you identify that may have colored your response?

• In what ways have you noticed society becoming less objective and more subjective?

QUICK DEFINITION

Today's lesson discusses existentialism, which is the belief that a person's life choices ultimately define his or her existence. Giving meaning to life comes from the individual because God does not exist.

THE VIEW REVIEWED

Tell the rest of the group what insights you gained from doing the "View of Your World" activity from the last lesson.

A VIEW OF OUR WORLD *(30 minutes)*

LISTEN TO TRACK 4 OF THE CD. In this BreakPoint segment, which aired June 1, 2001, Chuck Colson discusses how the preoccupation with self is negatively influencing our decisions.

BREAKPOINT EXERCISE

• Discuss the spread of the "selfist philosophy." How is this impacting our culture?

• In what ways is the selfist philosophy influencing our churches?

WATCH VIDEO SEGMENT 4. In this video, Chuck Colson talks about existentialism.

• Describe how existentialism elevates free choice and how that affects culture, values, and society.

• In what ways does existentialism threaten a Christian worldview? What is the Christian response to existentialism?

"If God does not exist, there is at least one being in whom existence precedes essence, a being who exists before he can be defined by any concept, and...this being is man...First of all, man exists, turns up, appears on the scene, and, only afterwards, defines himself."
—JEAN-PAUL SARTRE

Read the quotation from Jean-Paul Sartre, and discuss these questions:

• In what ways can we see man taking the place of God in pop culture?

• How has existentialism led to epidemic consumerism, the elevation of self, and the idea of subjective truth in our society?

THE VIEW FROM SCRIPTURE *(30 minutes)*

Read Philippians 2:1-18.

1. For the existentialist, ultimate truth comes from one's own understanding of life. Where does the Christian's ultimate truth come from?

2. How are Jesus' attitudes and actions the antithesis of existentialism?

3. Theoretically, how would putting self first lead to the destruction of sound Christian doctrine and practice?

4. How does the kind of conceit that comes from existentialism harm the body of Christ? At what point do our own personal interests, opinions, and convictions become improper?

5. Reflect on Christ's example in this passage. What is a Christian alternative to existentialism?

6. How can Christians counter existentialism and promote a Christian worldview to the world? What strategies should we employ to make a Christian worldview attractive to a culture enamored of self?

WRAPPING UP *(15 minutes)*

Consider the following list. Working individually, prioritize the list as you think an existentialist might. Then prioritize the list as you think a Christian would. Tell the group about your insights from this exercise.

	Existentialist	Christian
God	_____	_____
Self	_____	_____
Family	_____	_____
Boss	_____	_____
Culture	_____	_____
Career	_____	_____
Civil law	_____	_____
Duty	_____	_____
Freedom	_____	_____
Life's purpose	_____	_____
Extended family	_____	_____
Responsibility	_____	_____

As a group, discuss some of the blessings and curses that come with living in a time when we have many more personal choices than previous generations. In what ways do you live in an environment that breeds a "what's in it for me" mentality? What can you do to change culture?

PRAYER TIME

CLOSE YOUR SESSION IN PRAYER. Be sure to take the time to pray for each other. You may want to list prayer requests below so you can pray for each other during the week.

A VIEW OF YOUR WORLD

Watch a talk show of your choice. How much selfist philosophy can you discern? Look for standards of morality, definitions of family, remedies for life's struggles. During the week, try to be more aware of how the media may be directing your focus to your own personal wants rather than to the needs of others. Reflect on what choices you are making out of convenience that may be affecting someone else's needs this week. Make a conscious effort to find a way to help someone in need.

Is There More Than One Path to God?

GETTING STARTED *(15 minutes)*

Find a partner. Choose who will be the Christian and who will be the next-door neighbor. Read the following scenario, and spend a minute or two role-playing. Then switch roles so you both have an opportunity to practice articulating your beliefs about Christianity.

ROLE-PLAYING SCENARIO

You have known your next-door neighbor for five years but have not had many conversations. You have been praying for your neighbor, hoping to share your faith at the right time. Today your conversation goes deeper. Your neighbor says he is a Christian, but shares that he has been seeing a spiritual advisor, who performs something called "soul brightening" and reads "angel cards," a type of tarot card, during the sessions. He mentions his love for Jesus, angels, and fairies—all in the same breath. What would you say to clarify the gospel, although your neighbor believes he is a Christian?

Next take a few moments to reflect on how you would share your faith with your actual neighbors, and write down what you believe are the essentials of the Christian faith. After you have discussed them with your partner, share with the entire group what you came up with.

Today's lesson discusses the New Age movement, which is based on Eastern influences and pantheism—the belief that God is in all things. All people have God in them, therefore we all have the ability to be our own gods.

THE VIEW REVIEWED

Tell the rest of the group what insights you gained from doing the "View of Your World" activity from the last lesson.

A VIEW OF OUR WORLD *(30 minutes)*

BREAKPOINT EXERCISE

LISTEN TO TRACK 5 OF THE CD. In this BreakPoint segment, which aired August 24, 2001, Chuck Colson discusses the New Age trends of our day. New Age beliefs and techniques can be easily found in medicine, business, education, and even churches.

• What New Age beliefs, practices, or products have you encountered in our culture? What do they claim to offer?

• Why are these beliefs, practices, and products appealing to society? .

WATCH VIDEO SEGMENT 5. In this video segment, Chuck Colson discusses the New Age movement.

• Why do people feel that the New Age movement will lead them to God?

• Christians today are pegged as being intolerant and hostile toward other faiths. How can we respond to this criticism? Is God intolerant?

❝*We are Creating energy, matter and life at the interface between the void and all known creation. We are facing into the known universe, creating it, filling it...I am 'one of the boys in the engine room pumping Creation from the void into the known universe; from the unknown to the known I am pumping.'* ❞
—JOHN LILLY

Read the quotation from John Lilly, and discuss these questions:

• For Lilly, imagination is the same as reality. Everything that can be imagined, exists. What essential truths of Christianity are violated in this quote?

• How are people making their own religions, even in Christian circles?

THE VIEW FROM SCRIPTURE *(30 minutes)*

Read Exodus 20:1-5.

1. Why do people seem to want to believe there are other ways to God or other gods to believe in? Why does God demand that we worship only him?

2. Why do some people find the philosophies of the New Age movement so enticing?

Read John 14:6 and Acts 4:12.

3. How do these passages radically oppose New Age thinking? How can we respond to those who feel there are many truths?

Read Ephesians 4:14-15 and 2 Timothy 4:2-5.

4. How can Christians guard against New Age beliefs creeping into their lives? How can we be better prepared to give an answer for what we believe about faith?

5. Why is there only one way to God? How can we live out this truth in ways that will attract a nonbeliever to the gospel?

6. In our society, those who claim to know absolute truth are often branded as intolerant and hateful. How can we live out truth in our society?

Wrapping Up *(10 minutes)*

Brainstorm as a group what the gods of other world religions claim to offer that Christianity does not. List them on a dry-erase board or sheet of newsprint. Make another column, listing what Christianity offers us that other gods cannot.

Then pray together, praising God for who he is and what he does for us. Praise God for being the only true God, and praise him for his perfect plan of sending his Son Jesus to save the world from sin.

PRAYER TIME

CLOSE YOUR SESSION IN PRAYER. Be sure to take the time to pray for each other. You may want to list prayer requests below so you can pray for each other during the week.

A VIEW OF YOUR WORLD

Christians should make efforts to befriend non-Christians because we are called to go and make disciples in our world. Making friends with non-Christians can benefit us Christians. It's easy to take for granted all of the benefits salvation brings to our lives and forget what it's like to live without God. A non-Christian can serve to help sharpen our thinking about culture as Christians and give us greater compassion for the lost.

Do you have at least one non-Christian friend? If not, pray for God to help you develop a friendship with someone who does not know Christ. Before the next session, purposefully include a non-Christian in your circle of relationships.

What Is the Truth About Truth?

GETTING STARTED *(15 minutes)*

On an index card, write a statement that makes some type of claim or declares a truth—for example, "Jesus loves me," "All men are created equal," or "The sun always rises in the east." Put the index cards in a pile, and have the leader collect them and pass them out. Make sure you don't get your own card back. Then discuss the following questions.

• Do you believe this statement is true? How do you know? Can you prove that it is true or false?

• Is there such a thing as absolute truth? How do you know?

• Does our culture accept the idea of absolute truth? Why or why not?

Today's lesson discusses postmodernism, which is a worldview that dismisses the idea of universal truth as a type of oppression and concludes that there is no transcendent truth.

A postmodernist world resists not only Christian truth but rebels against any truth claims. Society is shaped by class, gender, and ethnicity.

THE VIEW REVIEWED

Tell the rest of the group what insights you gained from doing the "View of Your World" activity from the last lesson.

A VIEW OF OUR WORLD *(30 minutes)*

BREAKPOINT
EXERCISE

LISTEN TO TRACK 6 OF THE CD. In this BreakPoint segment, which aired January 11, 2002, Chuck Colson talks about the prevalence of lying and connects that with the rise of postmodern thought.

• What evidence do you see that indicates our culture has abandoned the ideas of absolute truth and absolute morality? Why is absolute truth important to Christianity?

• How has the abandonment of absolute truth and morality made itself evident within the church?

CULTURE
WATCH

WATCH VIDEO SEGMENT 6. In this video, Chuck Colson discusses post-modernism.

• In what ways is postmodernism negative? In what ways is it positive?

• How does a postmodern culture make it more difficult for people to embrace the truth of Christianity?

QUOTE,
UNQUOTE

"The very idea of freedom presupposes some objective moral law which overreaches ruler and ruled alike. Subjectivism about values is eternally incompatible with democracy...if there is no Law of Nature, the ethos of any society is the creation of its rulers, educators, and conditioners."
—C.S. LEWIS

Read the quotation from C.S. Lewis, and discuss these questions:

• What do you think Lewis is saying in this quotation?

• How does subjectivism about truth and values harm society? How does it harm Christianity?

THE VIEW FROM SCRIPTURE *(30 minutes)*

Read Exodus 20:1-17.

1. Christians, Jews, Muslims, and even Buddhists can agree to the tenets found in the Ten Commandments. How does God's law relate to general moral truths, which protect life, provide societal order, and preserve the family, whether Christian or non-Christian?

2. What truths about God are established in the Ten Commandments?

3. How do the Ten Commandments and other biblical teachings directly threaten popular postmodern culture?

4. Should Christians expect society to follow the absolute moral truth of the Ten Commandments? Why or why not?

5. Can you have law and order in society without a belief in absolute truth? How can Christians propagate absolute truth in a pluralistic society?

6. Read John 14:6. How can truth lead us to salvation? What was Jesus communicating when he referred to himself as truth?

7. How do we convince a postmodern world that God, as revealed in Scripture, is the source of absolute truth?

WRAPPING UP *(15 minutes)*

As Christians we know that we are saved by grace through faith in Christ and that having a relationship with God is much more than following a moral code or believing in absolute truths. However, it is good to be reminded that God's standard for truth is often the less popular choice in today's world.

Suppose that you have the ear of the entire world. You have five minutes to convince them of the absolute truth of Christianity. Summarize what you'd say during your five-minute oration, and tell the rest of the group.

PRAYER
TIME

CLOSE YOUR SESSION IN PRAYER. Be sure to take the time to pray for each other. You may want to list prayer requests below so you can pray for each other during the week.

A VIEW OF YOUR WORLD

Continue to meditate on the Ten Commandments through the week, and supplement your other Bible reading with Exodus 20:1-17. Reflect on how these ten laws are implicitly found in other Scriptures you read through the week. Did you feel you outwardly displayed a greater commitment to God's truth this week? If so, what opposition did you encounter?

CounterCultural Christians • PARTICIPANT GUIDE

Why Does Creation Matter?

GETTING STARTED *(15 minutes)*

Work together as a group to see if you can remember what God created on each day of Creation. When you're finished or after you've worked for five minutes, check your work against Genesis 1. Then discuss these questions:

• What does the world around us tell us about God?

• How does the doctrine of Creation help us to better understand our faith? our world?

QUICK DEFINITION

Today's lesson discusses Creation, which teaches that God is the source of all there is. Creation is the work of the triune God as we find in Genesis 1, which occurred by God's Word.

A VIEW OF OUR WORLD *(30 minutes)*

**BREAKPOINT
EXERCISE**

LISTEN TO TRACK 7 OF THE CD. In this BreakPoint session, which aired
August 29, 1995, Chuck Colson discusses Creation and the big-bang
theory.

• Do you think it's possible to be a creationist and also believe
in the big bang? Why or why not? Does the big-bang theory support
the doctrine of Creation in any way? Explain.

• What scientific facts support Creation?

**CULTURE
WATCH**

WATCH VIDEO SEGMENT 7. In this video, Chuck Colson emphasizes the
importance of the doctrine of Creation in the life of a Christian.

• Why should a Christian begin with the doctrine of Creation?

• How does nature teach us about God's love for us?

" *The marks of design are too strong to be got over. Design must have had a designer. That designer must have been a person. That person is GOD.* **"**
—WILLIAM PALEY

Read William Paley's quotation and discuss these questions.

• Do you agree that the design of the world leads one to believe in a designer? Why do some struggle with this idea?

• Why is God as creator pivotal to understanding his relationship to the world and toward humanity?

THE VIEW FROM SCRIPTURE *(30 minutes)*

Read Genesis 1:1; Psalm 33:8-9; Jeremiah 10:12; and Colossians 1:16-17.

1. Why is the doctrine of Creation so important?

2. What happens to a Christian's thoughts, belief, and faith if he or she chooses not to believe in Creation as described in Genesis?

Read Romans 1:25.

3. How do you see this verse coming true in our society? Why do people reject the evidence of creation and what it says about God?

Read Acts 17:16-32.

4. What does creation tell us about God?

5. How did Paul use the doctrine of Creation to evangelize non-Christians? How can we adapt Paul's strategy in our world?

6. How can we change the world by promoting the doctrine of Creation?

WRAPPING UP *(15 minutes)*

Take a piece of modeling dough, and make a representation of an object in nature that particularly declares the glory of God to you. Share with the group why you see God in the object you chose.

PRAYER TIME

CLOSE YOUR SESSION IN PRAYER. Be sure to take the time to pray for each other. You may want to list prayer requests below so you can pray for each other during the week.

A VIEW OF YOUR WORLD

Take a hike in nature to spend some quality time with God. Observe the intricate details of nature around you. Note new observances that you had not noticed before. What new insights did you gain about God's creative design? Did you sense a stronger connection with God away from man-made objects? Was it easier to worship?

Aren't People Basically Good?

GETTING STARTED *(15 minutes)*

On a sheet of paper, sketch a picture or a symbol that communicates to you the reality of sin in our world. Share your sketch with the group, and explain why you chose to illustrate sin in this particular way. Then discuss the following questions.

• Do any of the illustrations reflect the consequences of sin?

• Do you think you are sensitive to sin around you, or do you find it easy to ignore?

• Does your natural inclination lean toward seeing the good or bad in people around you? Why do you think that's so?

Today's lesson discusses the Fall of man, which is the doctrine that sin entered the world through Adam and Eve's disobedience, which brought about spiritual, social, and physical deprivation to the world.

THE VIEW REVIEWED

Tell the rest of the group what insights you gained from doing the "View of Your World" activity from the last lesson.

A VIEW OF OUR WORLD *(30 minutes)*

BREAKPOINT
EXERCISE

LISTEN TO TRACK 8 OF THE CD. In this BreakPoint segment, which aired September 15, 1999, Chuck Colson discusses the doctrine of the Fall.

• Why is the doctrine of sin particularly foundational to fully understanding the gospel?

• How has society's denial of the Fall affected the world? How has it affected the church?

WATCH VIDEO SEGMENT 8. In this video segment, Chuck Colson explains the need for Christians to understand the goodness of God in the midst of the evil effects of sin.

• How can we reconcile the goodness of God with the presence of evil in the world?

• How has sin and the Fall affected the world?

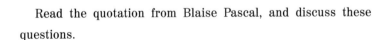

QUOTE, UNQUOTE

" *Certainly nothing offends more rudely than this doctrine [of original sin], and yet without this mystery, the most incomprehensible of all, we are incomprehensible to ourselves.* "

—BLAISE PASCAL

Read the quotation from Blaise Pascal, and discuss these questions.

• Does the doctrine of sin seem like a harsh reality to you? Is it a stumbling block to non-Christians you know?

• Consider what you've learned in the last seven sessions. What ideas and beliefs in our culture cause society to discount the idea that humans are inherently sinful?

THE VIEW FROM SCRIPTURE *(30 minutes)*

Genesis 1 and 2 depict man as a sinless being created in God's image with a free will. Read the account of the Fall in Genesis 3.

1. Satan used the tree of knowledge to tempt Eve. What can the tree be likened to in our world? What sly schemes can we see in the serpent's tempting words to Eve?

2. What evasive answers did Adam and Eve give to God when they were questioned? How do we continue to answer God in similar ways?

Read Romans 1:18-25 and 6:12-19.

3. What are the consequences of the Fall? How did the Fall have a cosmic scope in its effects?

4. Why must a moral and just God punish sin? How does God's punishment of sin and the redemptive work of Christ prove God's faithfulness to us?

Read Ephesians 2:1-10.

5. Describe the emotions this passage evokes in you. What does this passage teach you about yourself and about God?

6. How can we explain the Fall to a world that denies the Fall?

WRAPPING UP *(15 minutes)*

Think of a time in your life when God extended grace to you in a way that was very personal. If you feel comfortable, briefly share that experience with the group and how it affected your view of sin and forgiveness?

Next, think of a time when you've extended grace to someone in your life. Briefly share that experience with the group along with what it taught you about sin and forgiveness.

PRAYER TIME

CLOSE YOUR SESSION IN PRAYER. Be sure to take the time to pray for each other. You may want to list prayer requests below so you can pray for each other during the week.

A VIEW OF YOUR WORLD

By reflecting on our sin, we become naturally more aware and sensitive to offenses we commit toward others and God. This week read the model prayer Jesus gave us in Matthew 6:9-15 each night before bed. Specifically ask God to reveal to you any sin that is keeping you from a closer relationship with him and others. Confess your sin openly to God. Write down your prayers. Seek out a friend this week, confess your sin, and ask for his or her prayers in the areas you are struggling with. At the end of the week determine if you felt you were better able to resist temptation. Did God reveal areas of sin in your life that you were not previously aware of? How did you experience God's grace in greater ways?

What Is Redemption and Why Does It Matter?

GETTING STARTED *(15 minutes)*

Share with the group where and when you first heard the gospel message.

• What events or circumstances did God use in your life to bring you to him?

Look up the word *redemption* in a dictionary.

• How does each of the definitions of the word *redemption* relate to the work Christ did on the cross for us?

QUICK DEFINITION

Today's lesson discusses redemption, which is a term closely associated with salvation. To redeem means to buy back. The term redemption reminds us that our salvation has been purchased at great personal cost because Christ gave up his life as a ransom, taking us out of captivity and restoring us to a state of freedom.

A VIEW OF OUR WORLD *(30 minutes)*

BREAKPOINT
EXERCISE

LISTEN TO TRACK 9 OF THE CD. In this BreakPoint segment, which aired April 4, 1996, Chuck Colson discusses the conversion of former atheist Bernard Nathanson.

• How did God use evil resourcefully in Nathanson's life? How can we use an issue like abortion as a way to lead others to the redemptive work of Christ?

• Why is it important that society has a clear understanding of what redemption is? What hinders society from knowing about or understanding redemption?

CULTURE
WATCH

WATCH VIDEO SEGMENT 9. In this video segment, Chuck Colson elaborates on the powerful work of redemption in his life.

• What was particularly meaningful to you about Chuck's conversion? Can you find parallels in Chuck's story with your own?

• What did it feel like when you first realized you were free from sin?

• Although most of us will not experience the darkness of a prison cell, what do we have in common with the prisoner?

QUOTE, UNQUOTE

"God judged it better to bring good out of evil than to suffer no evil at all."
—AUGUSTINE

Read the quotation from Augustine and discuss these questions.

• How does what Augustine said describe redemption?

• Do you view the present or past suffering in your life as a blessing or a curse? Explain.

• What do suffering and redemption have to do with one another?

THE VIEW FROM SCRIPTURE *(30 minutes)*

Read Mark 10:45; Galatians 3:13-14; 4:5-7; Ephesians 1:7; and Colossians 1:13-14.

1. What images come to mind when you think of the word *ransom*?

2. What is the "curse of the law" that Paul refers to in Galatians 3:13?

3. What do these verses teach us about God? about ourselves?

4. Why is the idea of redemption so hard for the world to understand and accept?

Read Romans 3:21-31.

5. What is the central thought that Paul is trying to communicate about justification?

6. We have many names for God in the Bible. What does the name *Redeemer* teach us about God's love for us?

7. Knowing what you now know about how society's worldview is different from a Christian worldview, what methods or arguments would you use to explain redemption to non-Christians?

Wrapping Up *(15 minutes)*

Pass around a gift box. Talk about what makes gifts appealing. What is our response to gifts we don't like? What is our response to gifts we need? Reflect on how you have responded to the gift of salvation. Are you allowing the gift of salvation to transform all areas of your life?

PRAYER TIME

CLOSE IN PRAYER. Be sure to take the time to pray for each other. You may want to list prayer requests below so you can pray for each other during the week.

A View of Your World

It's easy to take for granted the life we have in Christ. This week go out of your way to do a deed of kindness for someone you wouldn't usually extend kindness toward. Be sure to pray for the person, too. Note the reaction to your deed of kindness. Did you find your attitude toward them changed? How is your act of kindness similar to the redemptive work of Christ on our behalf? How is it different?

How Can I Change the World?

GETTING STARTED *(15 minutes)*

Make a quick list of public places you visited this week in your community. Note which places reflect a Christian worldview and which ones oppose it. Take a moment to review the list and consider aspects of your community that you would like to change. Share your ideas with the rest of the group. Then discuss these questions:

• Are you content with the cultural patterns of your community? How would you like to see your community change?

• In general, do you think Christians are visibly working in your community to promote positive cultural changes?

• Which statement do you find to be more true: "Pop culture is transforming Christians" or "Christians are transforming pop culture"?

Today's lesson explores Christian restoration. When we come to Christ, we find personal spiritual restoration, which occurs within the community of the church. From our own personal transformation, we then can help restore private and public virtue in all areas of life.

THE VIEW REVIEWED

Tell the rest of the group what insights you gained from doing the "View of Your World" activity from the last lesson.

A VIEW OF OUR WORLD *(30 minutes)*

BREAKPOINT EXERCISE

LISTEN TO TRACK 10 OF THE CD. In this BreakPoint session, which aired January 15, 2002, Chuck Colson discusses a true story of healing and restoration.

• What is restorative justice and what are its benefits?

• What does restoration have to do with the gospel?

WATCH VIDEO SEGMENT 10. In this video segment, Chuck Colson explains what it means to live out our salvation.

• What does Chuck Colson mean when he says that salvation goes beyond John 3:16?

• Do you agree that Christians should work to transform our culture? Why or why not? What methods would be appropriate or inappropriate? What is our goal in working to transform culture?

"*In nothing has the Church so lost Her hold on reality as in Her failure to understand and respect the secular vocation. She has allowed work and religion to become separate departments...She has forgotten that the secular vocation is sacred.***"**
—DOROTHY SAYERS

Read the quotation from Dorothy Sayers, and discuss these questions:

• How well do you think the church equips Christians to seek virtue in all areas of life? How does this affect our impact on non-Christians?

• In her book *Creed or Chaos,* Sayers also asks, "How can anyone remain interested in a religion which seems to have no concern with nine-tenths of his life?" What challenges does this question pose to you? to your church? to your neighbors? to society?

THE VIEW FROM SCRIPTURE *(30 minutes)*

Read Matthew 5:13-16 and 2 Corinthians 5:11–6:2.

1. How did Christ show his desire to redeem and restore human cultural patterns during his earthly ministry?

2. According to Scripture, what do you think our cultural mandate is?

3. How can we use culture to extend God's kingdom without compromising our beliefs as Christians? What biblical parameters can we use?

Read 1 Corinthians 10:23-33.

4. What can we learn from Paul's views on culture?

5. What cultural patterns can you identify that your church uses to attract non-Christians? Do you think this is a good thing or a bad thing, and do you think it is compatible with Christianity?

6. What can you do as an individual to transform culture? as a family? as a part of this group? as a church?

WRAPPING UP *(15 minutes)*

As a group, identify a public forum in your community that needs more of a Christian perspective. Determine what you could do as a group to be effective representatives of Christ in that forum.

PRAYER TIME

CLOSE YOUR SESSION IN PRAYER. Be sure to take the time to pray for each other. You may want to list prayer requests below so you can pray for each other during the week.

A VIEW OF YOUR WORLD

This week, log onto Prison Fellowship's Web site (www.pfm.org) to learn more about restorative justice. Read some of the testimonies of transformed lives and how Christians are deeply impacting the justice system. Put yourself in the position of a victim of crime. What emotional challenges might exist? Then think of the criminal. Should there be more focus on the victim or the offender? Is it our responsibility to restore the offender to the victim, the community, and to God? Has this method changed how you view criminals? How might you discourage crime in your neighborhood?

What Place Should the Arts Have in the World?

GETTING STARTED *(15 minutes)*

Read the following definitions of tonal and atonal music. Then listen to the sample of tonal and atonal music on the CD (track 11), and discuss the questions that follow.

DEFINITIONS

Tonal music is a term used to denote a system of music based on major and minor keys related to a central tonic note. In tonal music other notes are important based on their relationship to the tonic, and there are precise mathematical principles that govern what is "pleasing" and "musical." These principles, which celebrate the natural order of the universe, go back to the ancient Greeks.

In atonal music, introduced in the twentieth century, the idea of a central tone was abandoned. In atonal music a sequence of twelve notes may be played forward, backward, in inversion, or both backward and in inversion forms. While there are rules in atonal music, the music sounds dissonant, random, and illogical to the ear because all tones have equal strength and importance.

• What differences can you identify in music samples? How do the styles differ?

• What does the dissonance in modern music, the atonal scale, communicate to you? What does the harmony in tonal music communicate to you?

• What roles do the arts have in helping us understand God? ourselves? the world around us?

A VIEW OF OUR WORLD *(30 minutes)*

BREAKPOINT EXERCISE

LISTEN TO TRACK 12 OF THE CD. In this BreakPoint segment, which aired May 17, 2002, Chuck Colson gives a critique of modern art.

• How do you define *art*? Do you agree with the statement, "Art is whatever an artist says it is"? Why or why not?

• What conclusions can be drawn about Gunther von Hagens' worldview?

CULTURE WATCH

WATCH VIDEO SEGMENT 11. In this video segment, Chuck Colson expounds on why the arts should matter to Christians.

• Do the arts matter to you? Explain.

• As Christians, how are we to interpret art? What role should art have in our lives? in the world?

QUOTE, UNQUOTE

❝*Since Christians, artists as well as evangelists, have within them the power of the Holy Spirit, it is only logical to conclude that artists, who bring everything into captivity for Christ, write, just as they live, under the direction of the Holy Spirit...Their poems are not private; they are images incarnated for themselves and for the community in which they live.*❞
—JOHN LEAX

Read the quotation from John Leax, and discuss these questions.

• In what way are the "images" of Christian artists "incarnated for themselves and for the community"?

• Is it our role as Christians to drive "bad art" out of our culture? Why or why not? How can Christians transform the art world?

THE VIEW FROM SCRIPTURE *(30 minutes)*

Read Psalm 19:1-4a.

1. What does God's artwork communicate to us and the world?

2. What does it mean to you to think of God as an artist?

Read Exodus 31:1-11 and 1 Samuel 16:14-23.

3. How was Bezalel's art and skill a spiritual calling? In what ways are Christians called today to create art? What should characterize the art created by Christians?

4. How was God present in David's music? How is God present in the art Christians create?

Read Philippians 4:8; 1 Corinthians 10:23; and 2 Corinthians 10:2-5.

5. What guidelines should Christians use when deciding what cultural entertainment to take part in and what to stay away from?

6. What does it mean to "take captive every thought"? How does this apply to Christians and the arts?

7. How can Christians influence the world through art? How can Christians transform the art world?

WRAPPING UP *(15 minutes)*

Describe a painting or a song or some other artistic work that has made a profound impact on you. Tell the group why the piece of art resonated with you. Talk about how the piece of art affected your emotions, your thoughts, and your actions.

PRAYER TIME

CLOSE YOUR SESSION IN PRAYER. Be sure to take the time to pray for each other. You may want to list prayer requests below so you can pray for each other during the week.

A View of Your World

This week make a point to read a piece of literature that requires some extra analysis, discipline, or thought to understand. You may want to read *Mere Christianity; The Lion, the Witch, and the Wardrobe;* or the *Screwtape Letters,* which are all written by C.S. Lewis. You may also want to read poetry by T.S. Eliot—try *Ash Wednesday* or *Four Quartets.* Another good work is Robert Louis Stevenson's *Treasure Island.* Look for the redemptive themes, and note what truths and images impacted you.

What Place Should Education Have in the World?

GETTING STARTED *(15 minutes)*

Think about your favorite teacher in grade school or high school. Share with the group why that teacher was your favorite and what you admired about him or her. Then choose one of these questions to answer and share with the group:

• Overall, did you have a positive experience in school? Explain.

• What did you value about your education? What would you change?

• Did the worldview presented in your school complement what you were taught at home?

A VIEW OF OUR WORLD *(30 minutes)*

BREAKPOINT EXERCISE

LISTEN TO TRACK 13 OF THE CD. In this BreakPoint segment, which aired May 22, 2002, Chuck Colson gives a disturbing account on the truth about science and education.

• Does welcoming representation from different worldviews enhance education? Why or why not?

• Do you think, generally speaking, that Christians are less informed about cultural influences in education than non-Christians? Explain. How can we improve the quality of thinking among Christians?

WATCH VIDEO SEGMENT 12. In this video segment, Chuck Colson examines the current condition of our educational systems.

• Do you agree that there has been a decline in academic training and moral education? Why or why not? If you do agree, what do you think has caused that decline?

• According to Thomas Aquinas, education should develop the God-given capacity to know what is true and good. How would you define education? What is its purpose in our lives?

QUOTE,
UNQUOTE

"Nonsense draws evil after it...We can therefore pursue knowledge as such, in the sure confidence that by so doing we are either advancing to the vision of God ourselves or indirectly helping others to do so...The intellectual life is not the only road to God, nor the safest, but we find it to be a road, and it may be the appointed road for us."
—C.S. LEWIS

• How has your education proven to be a road leading to God? Can the pursuit of knowledge ever lead us away from God? Why or why not?

• How does ignorance make us vulnerable as Christians?

THE VIEW FROM SCRIPTURE *(30 minutes)*

Read Deuteronomy 6:6-8 and Matthew 22:37.

1. How can we love God with our minds? What implications does that have for education? How can we better connect knowledge with our behavior?

Read Proverbs 1:7 and Colossians 2:2-4.

2. What does it mean to say "the fear of the Lord is the beginning of knowledge"? Why is it important to begin with Christ as the foundation of all truth?

3. Augustine believed that love for learning is directly linked to the desire for God. How can we better integrate our pursuit of knowledge with faith?

Read Proverbs 2:1-15 and Ecclesiastes 1:12-18.

4. Note what is similar and what is different in these passages. It's possible that Solomon wrote both of these passages. How could one man hold such different views?

5. Do you feel education is appropriately valued in our society? Why or why not? How should a Christian view education?

6. Does the church have a responsibility to educate its people? Why or why not? What role or responsibility do you think the church has in regard to education in our society?

7. What should Christians do, if anything, when society's educational system doesn't acknowledge God? What can Christians do to transform education?

WRAPPING UP *(15 minutes)*

In the book *The Fabric of Faithfulness: Weaving Together Belief and Behavior*, author Steven Garber writes that three factors stand out in successful Christian graduates: an integration of convictions, character, and community. On a scale of one to ten, rate your overall educational experience. If you have children, rate their experience, too. Share your opinion with the group. Then discuss these questions.

• Do you feel the three factors above were present in your education?

• Did you struggle with integrating your faith with learning?

• How can we better promote integrative thinking in public and private schools?

PRAYER TIME

CLOSE YOUR SESSION IN PRAYER. Be sure to take the time to pray for each other. You may want to list prayer requests below so you can pray for each other during the week.

A VIEW OF YOUR WORLD

Do a Web search on the history of education to learn how past generations viewed education and learning. What did you learn about the strengths and weaknesses of past generations? What are some of the strengths and weaknesses of education today? Note how your definition of education changed or was influenced by past academicians.

Help us provide you with quality worldview resources!

Thanks for using our worldview curriculum, *CounterCultural Christians*. We hope this product has been useful for you as you explore how to put your faith into action and as you disciple and mentor others in their faith.

In order for us to provide you with resources and products that can help you in your ministry, please take a few moments to complete this questionnaire and return it to us. To thank you for your time, we will send you one of our "Sources" publications.

Name _____ _____

Address _____

City _____

State _____ ZIP _____

Phone _____

E-mail _____

How are you using this curriculum (Sunday school, small group, etc.)?

_____

What was the age group of the students in your *CounterCultural Christians* class (teen, college, young adult, adult)?

_____

What other worldview resources would you use?

_____

_____

_____

___ I would like information about BreakPoint Worldview Magazine.

___ I would like information about Worldview Conferences.

___ I would like additional information about The Wilberforce Forum.

___ Sign me up to receive FREE daily BreakPoint Commentaries via e-mail.

What is your church affiliation?

_____

_____

Comments/Suggestions: _____

_____

_____

_____

For further resources, visit our Web site at

www.breakpoint.org

Photocopy pages 87-88 and mail to:

The Wilberforce Forum
1856 Old Reston Ave.
Reston, VA 20190

The Wilberforce Forum is a division of Prison Fellowship Ministries. The mission of The Wilberforce Forum is to catalyze the church's development of a Christian worldview for the 21st century, and to resource and sustain Christians as they engage the culture to transform it for Jesus Christ. Founded by Charles Colson, The Wilberforce Forum produces the daily BreakPoint radio program heard by over 5 million people on more than 1,000 outlets, conducts worldview conferences, and produces books and study guides on worldview issues. To learn more about The Wilberforce Forum or BreakPoint, visit www.wilberforce.org or www.breakpoint.org